THE DREAD OF LOVE

LOVE IS BEAUTIFUL AND SO IS THE PAIN

SHWETA SARTHY

FOR THE PEOPLE WHO SHOWED ME WHAT REAL LOVE AND FRIENDSHIP IS. WHO MADE ME REALISE WHO I AM IN REAL!!

!! I LOVE YOU !!

Contents

Contents

Foreword

"THE DREAD OF LOVE" A DARK ANTHOLY BOOK FILLED WITH AGONY AND GRIEF BUT AT THE SAME TIME BEAUTIFUL AND CHERISHING MEMORIES OF THE LOVED ONES. PEOPLE MAY TELL YOU HOW BEAUTIFUL LOVE CAN BE, THEY MAY TEACH YOU HOW TO LOVE PEOPLE BUT NO ONE EVER WOULD TEACH YOU HOW TO UNLOVE SOME PEOPLE OF OUR LIVES. IT'S NOT EASY TO UNLOVE TOO BUT THE THOUGHT OF TRYING TO UNLOVE SOME OF THEM WOULD ACTUALLY REDUCE THE SUFFER, PAIN GRIEF AND MISERY FROM US TILL AN EXTEND.

He used to make my heart throb like day with rain and sunshine...
easy to breathe, easy to smile and easy to live.
Look what he did to me now, keeping self in detention for something
i never did and still carrying regrets...
- shweta.s

Preface

MOST OF THE THINGS RECORDED IN THIS BOOK ACTUALLY OCCURED WHILE SOME WERE THE IDEAS HOW LIFE COULD BE. HOW LOVE COULD BE WHEN THE LIFE ITSELF IS A ROLLERCOASTER FILLED WITH UNEXPECTED SURPRISES.

Acknowledgements

NO ONE BUT MYSELF. I WOULD LIKE TO THANK MYSELF FOR NOT LOSING HOPE WHEN PEOPLE AROUND SAID WRITING IS A WASTE OF TIME. WHEN PEOPLE AROUND TRIED FORCING THEIR DECISIONS ON ME WHILE I KEPT DOING WHAT WAS NECCESSARY FOR ME. ALSO I WOULD LIKE TO THANK MY FATE WHICH LET ME FIND MYSELF THROUGH THE STORMS.

Prologue

THE THINGS THAT I WROTE IN THIS BOOK HAS NOTHING TO DO WITH ME. I NEVER EXPERIENCED LOVE NEITHER A HEARTBREAK. SOME PEOPLE JUST NATURALLY HAVE THE TALENT TO WRITE THINGS UP WITHOUT EVEN WITNESSING IT. I'M ONE OF THOSE. LOL

1. OCEAN WAVES

YOUR EYES WERE SAME AS THE WAVES
BLUE, BEAUTIFUL AND PROVISIONAL
MY HEART DESIRED TO SINK
BUT ONLY YOU WEREN'T ENOUGH TO STAY
WHY MAY THE SKY GOT TO OFFEND
WHEN THE UNIVERSE ITSELF KNEW
IT WASN'T THE OCEANS, SKIES OR THE MOON
BUT ALWAYS YOU AND YOU ALL OVER AGAIN
THE NIGHT WHEN I ACHED WITH UNDEFINED LONGING
OF YOU
YOU STAYED BESIDE AS THE ALLURE OF DARKNESS
ENFOLDED ME
WHEN MY SKIN CRAVED FOR YOUR TOUCH IN THE
DAYLIGHT
YOU CAME UP AS THE COLD BREEZE KISSED MY LIPS
THE ACHE PAST YOU
MADE ME FALL IN LOVE WITH THE POETRIES ALL AGIN
MAYBE WE AIN'T THE SAME WAVES ANYMORE
BUT DOES THAT MEAN WE AIN'T IN THE SAME OCEAN?
PERHAPS WE DON'T HAVE EVERYTHING SAME AS BEFORE
BUT DOES THAT MEAN EVERYTHING WE HAD BEFORE WAS
SURREAL?
- SHWETA S.

2. THE WILT FLOWER AMID PAGES

HOW AM I SUPPOSED TO APPRISE
WHAT YOUR LOVE INTENDS TO ME
YOU WERE THE WITHERED FLOWER
IN THE OLD SIDES OF MY FAV. BOOK
NO WONDER I STILL ADORE IT IN MY BOOK CASE
YOU WERE THOSE TINY GLINTING BIRDS
I USED TO GET EXHILARATE FOR, AFTER EVERY SHOWER
NO WONDER I STILL LOVE ADMIRING IT
YOU WERE THAT SHINY GLEAM OF SUN
AFTER THE CATASTROPH
TO LIGHT ME UP WITH THE GLEAM OF HOPE
YOU WERE THAT RATIONALE OF MY SECRET SMILE
UNDER THE VEIL WHEN I GLANCED AT YOU
NO WONDER I STILL DO REMEMBERING YOU
YOU WERE THE HAPPIEST STATE OF TIME
AND THE BELIEFS OF HAVING YOU ENTIRE LIFE
PHERHAPS THE FATE DIDN'T WANTED US TO BE A HAPPY
ENDING
BUT ATLEAST I SAW YOU DRIFTING AWAY
WITH A SMILE AND THAT'S WORTH IT
SHWETA .S

3. THE PLACE BEYOND EVERYTHING

THERE'S A PLACE BEYOND
RIGHT AND WRONG
A PLACE BETWEEN
THE CONDOUR AND LIES
A PLACE SO TINY
TO DIFFERENTIATE CHOICE AND FATE
A PLACE NOT TO JUDGE
& WOMEN NOT NEED SUFFRAGETE
A PLACE TO TALK ABOUT SILENCE
& APPRECIATE THE NON-FULFILLMENT
A PLACE BEYOND THE ACTUALITY
TO EMBRACE ONE'S TINIEST DREAMS
A PLACE TO LOOK BEYOND IMAGINATION
& EMOTIONS WITHOUT THEIR DEFINITIONS
A PLACE BEYOND THE QUESTIONS
TO ANSWER THE REALITY
FAR FROM CURBS AND MESS
WITH COFFEE AND GLIMPSES OF MOON
A PLACE WHERE YOU & ME TOOK OUR ORIGIN
PROBABLY NOTHING GT SAFER THAN THIS
SOBBING ON HER CHEST, FOR HOW CRUEL THE WORLD IS
BUT NOTHING GOTTA BE SAFER THAN HER LAP

4. WINGLESS BIRD

SHE WAS A BIRD WITH TINY WINGS
& THEY DECIEVED HER TO BE A WINGLESS BIRDS
SOMEHWERE IN THE BOWELS OF HER SOUL
LITTLE THAT SHE KNEW
WHO SHE ACTUALLY WAS
ALL HER LIFE SHE LIVED
WAS NOTHING BUT A LIE
SHE WAS A FAIRY GODMOTHER WITH SNIPPED WINGS
& THEY DECIEVED HER TO BE A WINGLESS BIRD
BUT LITTLE THAT SHE KNEW
SHE WAS SOMETHING DISCRETE
EVERYTIME SHE BASHED TO FLY
THE MANKIND SAPPED HER, CURTAILING TO FLY
HEWING WINGS WHILE SHE'S ASLEEP
TO DECIEVE SHE'S A WINGLESS BIRD
BUT LITTLE THAT SHE KNEW
THERE'S SOMETHING ATYPICAL
DECADES OF BEING A WINGLESS BIRD
MADE HER HEART DRIVER, SHE AIN'T ANYTHING SPECIAL
EVERYTIME SHE BASHED TO SOUR
SHE WAS SAPPED BACK TO EARTH
BY THE STRINGS LORE FOR WOMEN
BUT LITTLE THAT SHE KNEW
THE DREAM TO FLY HIGH

REMAINED A DREAM FOREVER
SHE WASN'T A WINGLESS BIRD
SHE WAS A GUARDIAN ANGEL
SENT TO EVOLVE THE MANKIND
BUT WAS COERCED TO STAY ON EARTH INSTEAD
WAS ITALL JUST BECAUSE
SHE WAS 'SHE' ....
- SHWETA.S

5. THE DARKEST NIGHT

AND THERE I WAS AGAIN AFTER A WHILE
ON THE SAME SHIP OF SORROW
DANCIN‘ AND FAKIN’ MY SMILE
TRYING TO FIGURE OUT THE FLOW
QUESTIONINGMY FATE BACK OVER
WHY WAS I ENCHANTED TO YOU?
AND WHAT ACHES THE MOST IF IT‘S OVER?
WHY DOES HIS PRESENCE STILL MAKES MY SORROW FLEW
YOU WERE MY MOON
IN THE DARKEST NIGHT
WHO MADE THIS FLOWER GLOOM
WITH HIS HOLY LIGHT
WHAT MADE US MEET IN THE SAME WAY?
WHILE WE WEREN’T MEANT TO BE
IS IT JUST MINE OR YOUR HEART SAYS THE SAME?
WAKIN' UP TO HAVE YOU BESIDE
IS IT TOO MUCH TO ASK FOR?
TO HAVE MY EYES SHINE BY YOU
IS IT TOO MUCH TO ASK FOR?
TO HAVE MY SOUL BESIDE YOU
- SHWETA.S

6. WOULD I EVER BE ABLE TO EXPLAIN?

I KNOW I CAN'T LET YOU GO
EVEN IF YOU ASK ME
WOULD I EVER BE ABLE TO EXPLAIN?
WHAT I REALLY HIDE INSIDE
IT'S STILL YOU, AND YOU AND ME HERE
PERHAPS BECAUSE WE NEVER LEFT
AND NEVER SAID GOOD BYE
THE SILENCE INSIDE
THAT BURNS YOU
THE UNSAID SINGLE WORD
THAT I HEARD MILES APART
THAT MADE US TURN OUR BACKS
FOR THE ONE LAST TIME
THAT PRO'LY CHANGED SOMETHING WITHIN US
OHH!! WAIT!!
AM I DREAMING THIS AGAIN
OR THIS IS FOR REAL!!
- SHWETA.S

7. BREEZE THAT KISSED ME

YOU WERE THE MOON THAT I COULD SEE
FAR FROM MILES APART
THE SUN ABOVE ME
THAT KEPT ME WARM
YOU WERE THE HAZED BREEZE
THAT KEPT ME ALIVE
THE OCEAN I WAS SCARED OF
THAT SAVED ME FROM DROWNING
YOU WERE THE STARS
THAT TWINKLED ABOVE ME
THE UNIVERSE AROUND ME
THAT BLOSSOMED ME EVERYDAY
IT WASN'T GOOD ENOUGH THOUGH
FOR THE MOON NOT TO BE REACHED
NOT THE SUN TO HEAL ME
BUT TO BURN EVERY INCH OF ME
AS THE HAZED BREEZE
THAT FLEW AWAY MY BLISS
AS MY DEEP BLUE OCEANS
THAT I'M AFRAID OF NOW
THE STARS ABOVE ALL
THOSE THAT SMILED WHEN I FAILED

BEING THE UNIVERSE ABOVE ME

AND NOT LETTING PEACE INTO MY FATE

- SHWETA.S

8. THE UNSENT LETTER

THE LOOK IN YOUR EYES WHEN YOU WERE DEEP IN YOUR THOUGHTS. OU LOOKED AWAY FROM MEAS YOU DIDN'T WANTED ME TO SEE YO CRY. THE WAY YOU WOULD HOLD MY HAND WHEN WE SAT BESIDE EACH OTHER. THE WAY YOU WOULD LOOK AT THE STRANDS OF MY HAIR AMID OUR CONVERSATIONS. THE WAY I USED TO LOOK FOR LOVE IN YOUR EYES AND EVERYTIME FOUND POETRIES IN THEM. LOVE DROPLETS ON MY FOREHEAD WHEN YOU TRIED KISSING THEM, I SAW YOUR EYES WEAKENING AND READY TO GIVE IN. HOW CAN I LET SOMEBODY READ YOU, ALL THAT THEY'LL FIND WILL BE ME IF THEY TRIED READING YOU. THEY WITNESS ME IN YOUR EYES. ME FOR THE PERSON YOU SHOWED ME I AM. ME FOR THE PERSON THAT WAS READY TO FALL APART IN YOUR ARMS. ME FOR THE PERSON THAT LET YOU SEE THROUGH MY BODY TO MY SOUL. ME FOR THE PERSON THAT SHOWED YOU HER DEEPEST SCARS. ME FOR THE PERSON WHO GOTTA BE STRONGER FOR THE REST OF THE WORLD FOR YOU BUT LETGO HERSELF WHEN WITH YOU. ME FOR THE PERSON THAT WAS WITH YOU AND ONLY YOU. ME FOR THE PERSON I WITNESSED MYSELF FOR THE FIRST IME. IT ACHES TO DEATH,HAVING SOMEONE AMID US, LETTING SOMEONE SIT BETWEEN US JUST TO MAINTAIN THE DISTANCE WE NEVER HAD, TO HAVE SOMEONE TO HOLD

US TOGETHER.

- SHWETA.S

9. HEAL

WHAT ARE THE CONSEQUENCES?
EVEN IF I CHANGE MYSELF
WHEN THE END HAS TO REMAIN SAME
BEING LEFT ALONE, ACCOPANIED WITH TEARS
WHAT'S THE POINT OF BEING MYSELF?
EVEN IF I TRY FINDING MYSELF
WHEN ALL I KNOW IS NOTHING ABOUT MYSELF
LEFT BACK AGAIN WITH MORE PUZZLED
WHY TO TRY FINDING PEACE IN OTHERS
WHEN I GOTTA STORM TO CALM IN ME
WHY TO TRY FINDING LOVE IN OTHERS?
WHEN I GOT SO MUCH TO LOVE IN ME
BUT STILL IN THE END
WE ALL ARE JUST STUPID HUMAN BEINGS
BEING DECIEVED BY SOMEONE ON THE IDEA
THAT LOVE AND ONLY LOVE
COULD HEAL US
WHEN ALL WE NEED IS COURAGE
TO LOVE WHO WE ARE
- SHWETA.S

10. STAND BY ME

FROM FIGHTING WITH EACH OTHER
TO STANDING WITH EACH OTHER
WE GREW UP TOGETHER
AVOIDING THE LOVE
GROWING WITH US AMID
YOU WANTED US TO BE FOREVER
AND SAID "PLEASE DON'T GO"
WHILE YOU WERE THE ONE LEAVING
PERHAPS ONE DAY, WE WLL MEET BACK
TO ACCOMPLISH THE INCOMPLETE STORY
IN THE WAY IT SHOULD BE
EVERYTHING WILL FALL IN PLACE ITSELF
AND WE WON'T BE FORCING ANYTHING
BUT RIGHT NOW, YOU'RE THE MEMORY
TIME COULDN'T ERASE
MY HEART STILL SEARCHES YOU
UNKNOWING THE FACT THAT
YOU LEFT WITHOUT A TRACE THIS TIME
- SHWETA.S

11. HOLD ON

HOLD ON I STILL WANT YOU
I WANT THAT LOVE BACK
I WANT THAT FRIENDSHIP BACK
I KNOW IT'LL BE HARD
BUT COMEBACK PLEASE
I WAS ALL LOST IN MY ASHES
BURNING DOWN YOU CASTLE
WHILE YOU WERE BUSY PRETENDING
THAT YOU NEVER CARED
HOW LONG WOULD YOU DENY
WHATEVER WE HAD
WHATEVER WE WERE
IT WAS ALL REAL
THE PAIN, LOVE, ANGER
IT WAS ALL REAL
IT WAS YOU WHEN I LIVED
IT WAS YOU WHEN I CRIED
IT WAS YOU WHEN I LAUGHED
AND IT WAS YOU WHEN I DIED
EYES AND HEART BEWILDERED
SOULD CRAVING FOR REINCARNATION
AND ALL ACHING AS HELL
- SHWETA.S

12. DOES IT HURT

WAS IT THAT EASY TO FORGET?
TO SHUTOUT WHAT WE HAD
AMID OUR SOULS
TO PASS OVER THOSE ENDLESS CONVERSATIONS
TO FORGET THOSE INEFFABLE EMOTONS
FOR A MOMENT ATLEAST SPARSE YOU EYES
DO WE REALLY DESERVE THIS?
DO THE PEOPLE DESERVE THIS WHO SAW FOREVER IN US
STAY A NIGHT MORE LOVE
I KNOW IT WAS OUR COMMITMENT
WHAT WASN'T IT TOO PROMPT?
THE BRAWLS, GIGGLES, THE BANTER
IT ALL WERE TO BE FOREVER
DO WE REALLY DESERVE TO HURT OURSELVES?
TO HURT OUR SOULS
THAT EXPECTED AN ETERNITY FROM US
WAS IT ALL THAT EASY TO SHUT OUT
TO FORGET WHAT WE PROMISED
IN THE CORE OF OUR HEARTS
TO FORGET THE INTIMAC THAT FLEW
THROUGH OUR EYES
FOR A MOMENT ATLEAST SPARSE YOUR EYES
AND ASK YOUR HEART
IS THIS HOW IT'S SUPPOSED TO END

WHY NOT GIVE A FORTUITY?
THIS LOVE MAYBE DARK
BUT ISN'T THE DARK BEAUTIFUL?
IT ALL MAYBE COMPLICATED
BUT AIN'T THIS ALL WORTH IT?
- SHWETA.S

13. CAN I SING YOU MY THOUGHTS

NO ONE WOULD HAVE EVER LOVED YOU THE WAY I DID
I WANTED TO MARCH IN
HOLD YOU TIGHT THERE IN
MY ARMSBUT ONLY WHEN
YOU COULD BREAK THOSE
WALLA AROUND YOU AND
LET ME IN!!
I WANTED TO BRING YOU BACK
ALIVE TO THIS WORLD
TO LIVE WITH YOU ECSTATICALLY
BUT ONLY WHEN YOU COULD
LET ME CLOSE TO THE COFFIN
OF YOURS!!
I WANTED TO SING YOU
ALL MY THOUGHTS
FOR THE LOVE I CARRY
IN MY HEART, BUT
ONLY WHEN YOU COULD
LET ME CLOSER ATLEAST!!
- SHWETA.S

14. HOW DO I LET GO?

BUT HOW DO YOU LET GO OF THE PERSON THAT FELT
LIKE HOME
AND WHY WOULD YOU LET GO SUCH A PERSON
ALL THAT PERSON SERVED YOU WITH
WAS PEACE AND HARMONY
AND LOVE AND HAPPINESS
THEY TOLD TO LET GO OF HIM
BUT DOES THAT MEAN TO LET GO OF MY BLISS TOO
TO LET GO OF THE PEACE THAT HE SERVED
THEY TOLD ME TO LET GO OF THE PERSON
WHO USED TO BE MY LIFE
SO DOES THAT MEAN, I GOTTA LET MY SOUL
OUT OF MY LIFELESS BODY TOO
BECUZ THAT'S WHAT IT MEANS
LETTING GO OFF THE PERSON
WHO USED TO BE NOTHING BUT EVERYTHING
IS WHAT YOU NEED TO KILL YOURSELF
LET GO THEM AND LET YOURSELF GO TOO
SO AS THE SOULS WERE MEANT TO BE TOGETHER
IRRESPECTIVE OF BEING ON EARTH OR CLOUDS
WE GOTTA FIND PEACE WHEREVER WE GO
BECUZ THAT'S WHAT WE NEED TO BE ETERNAL
TO MAKE US IMMORTAL
SO THE PEOPLE AFTER US GETS TO WITNESS US

15. I HOPE YOU CAN STILL FEEL IT

I HOPE YOU CAN STILL FEEL IT
I HOPE YOU STILL KNOW
THAT I AM HERE
DOWN ALONG THE LONELY ROADS
THROUGH THE DARK WET FORESTS
I AM STILL HERE
STANDING ALONG THE CEMETERY
ROAMING AROUND MY GRIEVESTONE
CARRYING THE HOPE IN ME
THAT YOU'D COME ONCE ATLEAST
CROSSING THE RIVERS AND OCEANS
IN STORMS AND DAYLIGHT
I HOPE YOU STILL FIND IT
MY LOVE ON THIS PLANET
FOR IT'S IMMORTAL
- SHWETA.S

16. HE STILL MAKES ME BLANK

YOU STILL MAKE ME NERVOUS
WHEN YOU WALK IN THE ROOM
AND INSTANTLY CATCH MY EYES
THE BUTTERLIES COMIG ALIVE IN ME
WHEN YOU SIT NEXT TO ME
YOU STILL RAISE MY HEART RATE
WHEN YOU SAY MY NAME
HAVING MY BRAIN WITH LACK OF THOUGHTS
WHEN I TURN BACK JUST TO FIND YOU CATCHING MY EYES
YOU STILL MAKE ME BLANK
WHEN THE TIP OF YOUR HANDS TOUCHES MINE
LEAVING MY SOUL SHIVER
WHEN YOU KISS ME SITTING
MILES AWAY FROM ME
- SHWETA.S

17. FOR ETERNITY

FOREVER AND EVER
WAS THIS ALL A NIGHTMARE?
A BEAUTIFUL NIGHTMARE OF ALL TIMES
WHILE THE REALITY CLICKED ME
WHEN I WANTED TO HOLD YOU CLOSER
IN THE SPACE WHERE MY SHADOW MEETS MY SKIN
IN THE PLACE WHERE MY SOUL KISSES YOURS
SO MUCH WAS SAID WHEN UNSAID
IF YOU WERE TOO SCARED TO SPEAK OUT
COME AND SIT BESIDE ME IN THE ROOF TOP
BENEATH THE MOON AND LET THE SILENCE CONFESS EVERYTHING
IT CLICKED ME THE VERY FIRST TIME
HOW BADLY IT'S GONNA HURT
LOSING YOU, THE WORSE
I COULD WRITE 1000S OF PAGES, FOR THE WAY YOU HURT ME
BUT OHHH!! WAIT!!!
I COULD ACTUALLY WRITE A NOVEL OR TWO, FOR THE WAY YOU LOVED ME
ALTHOUGH IT WAS ALL FOR A MOMENT
BUT I'LL KEEP IT DEEP INSIDE MY OUL TILL ETERNITY
- SHWETA.S

18. MAYBE

MAYBE IT WASN'T MEANT TO WORK BETWEEN US
MAYBE IT WASN'T REAL, ALL THAT WE HAD
MAYBE THE LOVE AMID US
WASN'T ,EANT TO BE ETERNAL
MAYBE THE LAUGH, THE MISERY, IT WAS ALL SURREAL
MAYBE THE DISTANCE AND THE INDIFFERENCE
WAS ALL THAT WAS REAL
MAYBE THE UNIVERSE DIDN'T LIKED
DIDN'T LIKED TO WITNESS US TOGETHER
OR MAYBE WE WERE JUST SIMPLY NOT MEANT TO BE TOGETHER
- SHWETA.S

19. I CHOSE YOU

OUT OF ALL THE FLOWERS, I CHOSE YOU
INSPITE OF THOSE SPINES
CUTTING ME INTO PIECES
THAT I COUL NEVER GAIN BACK MYSELF
I WAS BUSY EMBRACING YOU
SHUTTING OFF THE FACT
THAT IT ALL COSTS MY PEACE
TO LEAD YOU TILL THE BLISS
WHERE I WAS WISHING, AN ETERNITY TO SPEND
AND YOU PROVED THAT YOU WERE AMONG THEM TOO
TO SHED SKIN EVERY MOMENT FOR EVERYONE
- SHWETA.S

20. WHY DON'T YOU PROVE IT

YOU SAID YOU DON‘T LOVE ME
THEN WHY DON’T YOU PROVE IT
WHY DON‘T YOU SHOW ME
THAT YOU DON’T CARE AND NEVER DID
WHY DON‘T YOU SHOW IT THAT YOU HAVE MOVED ON
SO THAT I CAN WALK ON TOO
WHY DON’T YOU SAY IT THAT YOU DON‘T LOVE ME
AND ACTUALLY NEVER DID
REMEMBER THE LAST TIME WE MET
AND I SAID SOMETHING LIKE
"I’M NOT SCARED OF LOVE, I‘M SCARED OF
BEING THE ONLY ONE TO BE IN LOVE"
YOU KNEW IT BEFORE TIME BUT NEVER CONFESSED THE REAL YOU
AND NOW THAT YOU’RE HERE,
IT‘S BEEN TOO LATE DARLING!
IT’S BEEN TOO LATE TO LOVE YOU BACK
IT‘S BEEN TOO LATE TO WALK BACK
IT’S BEEN TOO LATE TO RETURN BACK ON EARTH
BUT LET ME TELL YOU LOVE, I‘VE ALWAYS LOVED YOU
I LOVED YOU WHEN I WAS THERE ON EARTH
I LOVED YOU WHEN I WAS ALIVE

AND I STILL LOVE YOU FROM THIS HEIGHT
AND I STILL LOVE YOU, SHUTTING OFF YOUR PAST
PERHAPS I'M DEAD BUT MY LOVE?
NAHH!! DARLING IT'S ETERNAL
I'LL ALWAYS BE WITH YOU
YOU WON'T BE ABLE TO SEE ME FOR I WON'T ME VISIBLE
BUT CLOSE YOUR EYES MY HUMAN,
YOUR SOULMATE IS JUST BESIDE YOU
CLOSE YOUR EYES AND FEEL ME
FEE MY EXISTANCE, FEEL MY PRESENCE, FEEL MY LOVE
AND FEEL ME
I'M RIGHT HERE BESIDE YOU,
HOLDING YOUR SOUL FROM FALLING APART
I'M RIGHT HERE!!!
- SHWETA.S

21. MAYBE ONE DAY

AND PERHAPS ONE DAY
HE'LL LOOK BACK ONCE
AT ME AND SAY
'GODDAMN SHE REALLY LOVED ME"
ANDTHEN I'LL TURN MY BACK ON
AND SAY
"THE GODDAMN GIRL IS STILL
INLOVE WITH YOU"
- SHWETA.S

22. THE COURAGEOUS HEART

INSECURITIES ARE GONE
AND SO DID PAIN
THE PATH PERHAPS STONED
BUT COURAGE, HEART HAS TO GAIN
SUNRISE AFTER A STORMS
CHILLED BREEZE AFTER RAIN
MORNINGS WITH SONNET POEMS
AND HEART THAT IS INSANE
GO BACK TO THE VERY BEGINNING
AND START OVER AGAIN
FATE MAY LET YOUR FEET TREMBLING
BUT DON'T LET IT BREAK THE HOPE OF CHAIN
IT MAY CAUSE YOU TEARS
WITH BLOOD AND AGONY
BUT DON'T LET YOUR HEART FEAR
SERVE IT WITH COURAGE AND HARMONY
YOU'VE LIVED AMID THE BITTERNESS
YOU'VE FACED THE IMPOSSIBLES
YOU LEARNT TO LIVE WITH THE LITTLENESS
AND SURVIVED THE HORRIBLES
- SHWETA.S

23. HIS FEEL

I FELT HIM LONG BEFORE WE ACTUALLY TALKED
I FELT HIS PRESENCE ALL AROUND
FOR I KEPT HIM DEEP INSIDE MY HEART
WRAPPED WITH BONES AND MUSCLES
HE WAS ALL THAT I HAD
WHILE I WAS JUST A SHADOW BEHIND
HE DREW ART AROUND MY SCARS AS IN
THE SCARS WERE ONCE MADE UP
JUST SO THAT HE COULD MAKE AN ART OF IT
HE FINELY DREW THEM AND LEFT ME
AS HIS ONLY MASTERPIECE
HIS BREATH, HIS LIFE, EVERYTHING
THAT WAS DRAWN IN THE ART
AND HE LEFT WITHOUT GLANCING BACK AT IT
WITHOUT TAKING HIS ART WITH HIM
HE LEFT...
- SHWETA.S

24. I CHOSE TO BE THE POET

WHEN I CHOSE TO BE A POET
IT WAS ME, WHO CHOSE
TO SOB THROUGH WORDS
TO BLEED THROUGH INK
TO DIE IN WILT PAGES OF ANCIENT BOOKS
WELL, I CHOSE TO BE THE MUSEUM
THAT DIED IN ITSELF FOR THE VIEWERS
WHO KNEW WHAT I WENT THROUGH
PEOPLE NEITHER ASKED, HOW THE MUSEUM IS
ALL THAT THEY DID WAS TO CHERISH
THE WORDS AND DEATH IN WILT PAGES
OF MINE AND MANY OTHER
WHO DIED YAERS BEFORE ACTUALLY BEING DEAD
WITH AN UNREVEALED LETTER OF LOVE
THAT WAS BURRIED DEEP UNDER THE INFRASTRUCTURES
- SHWETA.S

25. POETRY AND THE SPILLED WORDS

HE WAS A POETRY
WHILE EVERYONE MERELY WERE JUST WORDS
SHE WAS A FREE VERSE
WHILE EVERYONE AROUND WERE JUST
SOME RANDOM WORDS ASSEMBLED
THE NIGHT BEFORE WE MET
IT WAS NOTHING BUT ALL DARK
THE BACKYARD OF MY HEART
WHERE WAS BURRIED, THE LOVE
HE DRAINED IT ALL OUT
LIKE IT WAS ALWAYS HIS
THE LOVE, THE HEART, IT'S ALL HIS
- SHWETA.S

26. THE WHISPERS

YOU'RE MINE HE BREATHES
ALL YOURS AND SHE WHISPERS
LOOKING THROUGH THE FLESH
DIRECTLY TO THE CARDIAC ORGAN
THROBING AS NIMBLE AS HERS
AS SHE STRIDES CLOSE BY
HE CLOSED HIS EYES
ENGULFING THE SALIVA
AND ADMIRING HER LIPS
AND IT'S AURA
AS THEN HIS LIPS NUDGED HERS
HE OPENED HIS EYES
THAT GLANCED DIRECTLY INTO HERS AND MIEN
HIS EYES SAID EVERY SLIGHTEST THING
AND WHEN HE WINKED BACK
AND KISSED ME ZEALOUSLY
WITH POURING ALL HIS LOVE
ON HER...
CLUTCHING HER NECK AND PUSHING BACK
AGAINST THE WALL
WITH WAISTS AND CHESTS COLLIDED
ALL SHE EXPERIENCED WAS
THE AMOUNT OF FERVENT
YO HAVE HER, TO GET HER IN HIS ARMS

HOW EVERY MOMENT OF IT
APRRISED, HOW TERRIBLY HE WANTED HER...
- SHWETA.S

27. SUNSHINE & BROKENNESS

AND ONE FINE DAY
WHEN I TOOK HIS NAME
IT NO MORE FELT LIKE
FLOWERS AND SUNSHINE
IT WAS ALL DARK AND
NOTHING BUT BROKENNESS
BEING REVEALED FROM EVERY WORD
THAT CAME OUT OF MY MOUTH
HE USED TO THINK
THAT I LOVED THE BEACHES
FOR I LOVED THE BEACHES
ONLY WHEN HE WAS BESIDE
CAN WE STAR OVER EVERYTHING NOW?
AGAIN?
WITH A FRESH NEW BEGINNING
WITH NEW HOPES THIS TIME
YOU'D STEAL MY EYES AGAIN
AMONG THE CROWD AND
I'D STEAL YOUR HEART ONCE AGAIN...
- SHWETA.S

28. RAW PEACH

WHEN I KISSED HIS LIPS
IT TASTED LIKE RAW PEACH
IT TASTED LIKE PEACE
EVERYTHING SEEMED SO QUIETUDE
AMID THE CATOSTROPHIC PHASE
THE KISS GOT US MUZZLED UP
BUT THE EYES VOCALISED ALL
THE MOMENT HIS LIPS MET MINE
IT ALL FELT LIKE JOUISSANCE AND GAIETY
I WAS ALL GIRDLED WITH HIS LOVE
SECURED AND ENSURED IN HIS ARMS
AND ALL I FELT THEN WAS HIS HEART THROBBING
EXACTLY TO MY EARS IN ADJACENT
ALL THAT MY HEART DESIRED THERE
WAS TO BE THERE FOR ETERNITY
AND WAS IT ALL TOO MUCH TO ASK FOR...??
- SHWETA.S

29. MAYBE FOR ONCE

BUT MAYBE JUST FOR THE MOMENT
LET ME LIVE IN THE FANTASY
LET ME WEAR THIS WHITE WEDDING GOWN
WHILE YOU WAIT FOR ME THERE DOWN
NO MATTER IF IT'S HURTING
I DO WANNA LIVE THIS MOMENT
PERHAPS IT'S JUST FOR ONCE
ONCE IN A LIFETIME
LET ME LIVE IN MY FANTASY FOR ONCE
KNOWING THAT YOU'LL BE GONE
YOU'LL BE GONE THE NEXT MORNING
LET ME BE YOURS FOR ONCE
LET ME FEEL IT ALL TOGETHER
FOR ONE LAST TIME
KNOWING THAT YOU'LL BE SOMEONE'S
THE NEXT MORNING
BUT MAYBE JUST FOR THE MOMENT
LET ME LIVE IN MY FANTASY
LET ME WEAR THIS WHITE WEDDING GOWN
AND RING YOU WITH A WIDE SMILE
KNOWING HOW IT ALL GONNA HURT
WHEN I TEND TO OPEN MY EYES
AND REALISE IT WAS ALL A DREAM
LET ME LIVE THIS MOMENT

NO MATTER IF IT'S HURTING
I DO WANA LIVE THIS MOMENT
PERHAPS FOR JUST ONVE
ONCE IN MY LIFETIME
LET ME LIVE IN MY FANTASY
KNOWING THE MOMENTS SPENT
WERE NOTHING BUT JUST A DREAM
FOR ONE LAST TIME
KNOWING THAT YOU'LL NEVER LOVE ME BACK
NOT IN THIS LIFE
BUT PERHAPS JUST FOR THE MOMENT
LET ME LIVE IN MY FANTASY
- SHWETA.S

30. THE GUARDIAN ANGEL

I MISS THE SOFTNESS OF HIS SKIN
AS HE USED TO PULL THE STRANDS
OF MY HAIRS,
TO THE BAXK OF MY EARS
I MISS HIS PERFUME
THAT USED TO STICK AROUND ME
AFTER A LONG HUG
I MISS MY SMILE
THAT I DISCOVERED
ONLY WHEN AROUND HIM
I MISS HIS HEART
THAT USED TO BEAT
FASTER AS SOON AS I TOUCH HIM
I MISS THOSE GRUMPY MESSY HAIRS
THAT MADE ME FALL FOR HIM
AT THE FIRST
I MISS THE REAL HIM
THAT ONLY I WITNESSED
THE WORLD MAY SEE HIM
AS A REGULAR HUMAN BEING
BUT WHO KNEW HE WAS
A GUARDIAN ANGEL FOR ME

31. I'M STILL HERE

I'M STILL HERE LOVE
YOU JUST GOTTA CALL OUT
LOOK OUT FOR ME,
I'M RIGHT HERE.
LOOK OUT IN THE DARK FORESTS
FOR ME, WHERE THE WILD WEED GROWS.
I'M RIGHT HERE,
LOOK OUT BENEATH THE GROUND
FOR ME, WHERE I'VE BEEN BURRIED FOR AGES
I'M RIGHT HERE.
LOOK OUT IN THE ASHES
THAT BURNT NEAR YOUR COFFIN
WHEN YO WERE GONE
I'M STILL RIGHT HERE.
LOOK OUT IN THE SKY
FOR ME, DEAR
I'VE BEEN LOOKING AT YOU
FROM THE CLOUDS,
I'M RIGHT HERE.
I WAS HERE AND I'VE BEEN HERE SINCE
THE DAY YOU LEFT, HOPING AND
INHALING EVERY BREATH
THAT COULD END UP AFTER WITNESSING YOU
ONE LAST TIME

32. F.R.I.E.N.D.S

WELL THEY MADE ME SMILE
WHEN I WAS ON THE VERGE
TO LOSE MYSELF
THEY STAYED BESIDE ALL THE WAY
WHEN I WAS BEING KNOCKED DOWN
WHEN I WAS BEING CHERISHED
THEY NEVER PROMISED TO SAVE ME
FROM ALL THE DOWNS AND TWISTS
IT WAS ALL IN FATE, AND IT WAS NECESSARY
BUT THEY KEPT THEIR PROMISE TO STAY
BESIDE EVERYTIME, EVERY SINGLE TIME
I GOT TO FACE MY FATE
THE BEST PHASE ABOUT LIFE
YOU KNOW WHAT IT IS?
IT'S WHEN THE FATE SUCEEDS IN
KEEPING YOUR LOVE AWAY BUT
NEVER IN KEEPING FRIENDS AWAY
PERHAPS BECAUSE, THE UNIVERSE KNOWS
FOR PEOPLE COULD STAY ALIVE WITHOUT LOVE
BUT FOR SURVIVAL, THERE'S ALWAYS A NEED OF FRIEND
- SHWETA.S

33. F.R.I.E.N.D.S 2

YOU TALK ABOUT LOVE
AND ALL MY MIND THINKS OF
IS F.R.I.E.N.D.S
THE ENDLESS LAUGHTER
UNTIL WE END UP WITH TEARS
IN EYES AND HANDS ON OUR STOMACH
THE DAYS WE USED TO MAKE OUT PLANS
BUT NEVER SUCEEDED IN IT THOUGH
WHAT ELSE IN THE WORLD
DOES ANYONE EVER NEED
WHEN YOU HAVE A FRIEND TO
BUY YOU PIZZAS EVERYTIME YOU FEEL LOW
FRIENDS THAT REACH UPTO YOU
JUST KNOW YOU'RE FINE
FRIENDS THAT KEEP YOU AWAY
FROM TOXICITY ALL THE WAY
ALL THE WAY TILL THE END
*WHO NEEDS A F***ING LOVE STORY*
WHEN YOU'VE GOT FRIENDS
- SHWETA.S

34. I COULD HAVE ASKED

YOU DO HURT ME STILL
BUT NOT AS MUCH AS I DO
BY STILL LOVING YOU
I STILL HOLD ON IN THE HOPE
THAT YOU'L COME BACK
PERHAPS ONE DAY ATLEAST
YOU MADE ME REALISE
HOW PRECIOUS THE TINY MOMENTS
COULD BE ATER YOU LOSE THAT 1 PERSON
THE LITTLE SHORT CLIPS
THAT RUNS THROUGH MY HEAD
RIGHT AFTER SEEING YOU
AND REALISING I COULD HAVE
ASKED YOU ONE MORE TIME
I COULD HAVE ASKED YOU
ONE MORE TIME TO STAY BACK
I COULD HAVE ASKED YOU
ONE MORE TIME TO SPEAK UP
I COULD HAVE HELD YOU BACK
ONE LAST TIME
PERHAPS THEN THE END WOULD HAVE CHANGED
- SHWETA.S

35. DAYLIGHT AND MOON

I WAS LYING ON MY BED
TRYING TO OVERCOME EVERYTHING
TRYING TO FIGURE OUT
ALL THAT I WENT THROUGH
LYING ON MY BED
AND HEAD BURRIED IN THE PILLOW
THE PILLOW THAT HAS ALWAYS BEEN THERE
WHEN I WAS IN TEARS
WHEN NO LIVING BEING DID
TRYING TO FIND MYSELF
A HOPE TO LIVE
I TRIED HEALING THE BROKENNESS
WHILE MY SOUL SHIVERED
EVERYTIME I TRIED STEPPING OUT
IF YOU WERE THE SUN
NIGHT IS ALL I COULOD EVER BE
IF I WERE THE MOON
DAYLIGHT IS ALL YOU COULD EVER BE
FOR WE'LL NEVER BE ABLE
SEE EACH OTHER BUT STILL BE IN LOVE
- SHWETA.S

36. FOR A MOMENT

FOR A MOMENT I THOUGHT
IT WAS ALL OVER
THE PEACE, HAPPINESS
THE LAUGHS AND GIGGLES
UNTIL I FELT SOMEONE
TAPPING ON MY SHOULDER
& WHEN I TURNED EXPECTING IT TO BE YOU
IT WASN'T YOU, BUT SOMEONE BETTER
SOMEONE WHO ACTUALLY DESERVED
THE LOVE I GAVE YOU
SOMEONE WHO ACTUALLY DESERVED
MY HEART TO OWN.
- SHWETA.S

37. I'LL BE THERE

I STILL LOVE YOU
EVEN IF WE END UP
NOT LIVING TOGETHER
EVEN IF THE WORLD
DOESN'T LET US FREE
EVEN IF THE FATE
DOEN'T LET US CLOSER
I'LL BE THERE
WAITING IN THE HEAVEN
I'LL BE THERE
TO SE YOU FREE OFF THE AGONY
I'LL BE THERE
AT THE PLACE, WHERE OUR SOULS
COULD GET CLOSER
EVEN IF THE FATE DOEN'T LET ME
I'LL STAND BY YOU
EVEN IN THE FIRE
HOLDING YOUR HAND BESIDE
UNTIL YOU'RE SET FREE
- SHWETA.S

38. ALL WE WANT

ALL WE WANT IN THE END
IS TO HAVE A PLACE
WITH THE PERSON
WHO FEELS SECURED AND LOVED
A PLACE APART FROM REALITY
YOUR OWN FANTASY WORLD
BUT THIS TIME
WITH THE RIGHT PERSON
BEFORE FALLING FOR YOU
I WANT TO FALL FOR THE MOMENT
WHEN I SAW YOU FOR THE FIRST TIME
UNKNOWING THE FACT
I'LL BE FALLING FOR YOU
IN YOUR EVERY SIGHT
- SHWETA.S

39. ROSES AND THORNS

WHAT MORE WORDS CAN I WRITE
TO DEFINE US, IF NOT THE
ROSES AND THORNS AND NOT THE
BREZZE AND STORM
AS I SAID, ONLY TWO CAN HAVE ME
ONE WAS HIM, THE OTHER WAS DEATH
PERHAPS THAT'S WHY
HE GAVE UP FOR THE DEATH
I KEPT MY PROMISE
TO COMEBACK FOR HIM
I CAME BACK AS WINDS, WATER AND TREES
BUT HE NEVER TRIED SEARCHING
HE NEVER TRIED SEARCHING
FOR MY TRACES,
SINCE THE HUMAN IN ME WAS DEAD
AND NOT THE LOVE
- SHWETA.S

40. *****

I STILL KEEP THE DOORS OPEN IN HOPE THAT PERHAPS ONE DAY, YOU'LL END UP STEPPING INTO MY WORLD, EVEN IF IT'S BY MISTAKE. IN HOPE THAT PERHAPS SOMEHOW, YOU'LL FIND PUT THE DAMAGE CREATED BY YOU AND HOW IT ALL HAS BEEN DARK AND LIFELESS AFTER YOU...

***

LET'S NOT LIE ANYMORE
FOR IT'S GETTING HEAVIER
LET'S JUST GET DRUNK ON THE FACT
AND PRETEND LIKELOVE IS FOR LOSERS
WHO AIN'T COURAGEOUS ENOUGH
TO LIVE WITHOUT LOVE
"LET'S NOT MAKE IT COMLICATED"

41. *****

YOU THINK A GRAVE CAN HOLD MY BODY DOWN AND SUCEED IN KEEPING IT AWAY FROM HIM? NAHH!! MY LOVE. I'LL SWIM TO HIM OR I'LL FLY TO HIM BUT BY ANY MEANS, I'LL REACH HIM.

***

"BUT HOW'D YOU KNOW HE'S THE ONE?" "HE ASKED ME EVERYTIME BEFORE HOLDING ME"

***

AND PERHAPS ONE DAY, HE WILL LOOK BACK AT ME FOR ONCE AND SAY, "GODDAMN, THE GIRL RALLY LOVED ME" AND THEN I'LL TURN MY BACK ON AND SAY, "THE GODDAMN GIRL IS STILL N LOVE WITH YOU"...

***

I TRIED ALL THE POSSIBLE WAYS I COULD TO RUN AWAY FROM YOU, DECEIVING THE FACT, THAT EVERY PATH OF MINE LEADS ME TO YOU...

I DON'T KNOW HOW EVERY SINGLE LINE AND WORD OF MY BOOK MADE YOU FEEL BUT I HOPE IT'D HAVE BEEN A GREAT EXPERIENCE. I LOVE YOU PEOPLE!!

Printed by Libri Plureos GmbH in Hamburg,
Germany